MW01300776

THIS BOOK BELONGS TO

CPSIA information can be obtained
at www.ICGtesting.com
Printed in the USA
BVHW040858230619
551730BV00015B/238/P

9 781072 573302